Critical Thinking Activities • Challenging

Brain Teasers

by Carol Eichel

Grades 5-8

Teacher Created Resources, Inc.
6421 Industry Way
Westminster, CA 92683
www.teachercreated.com

ISBN: 978-1-55734-491-5

©1993 Teacher Created Resources, Inc.
Reprinted, 2009

Made in U.S.A.

Edited by
Amy LasCola

Illustrated by
Keith Vasconcelles

TABLE OF CONTENTS

INTRODUCTION

Brain Teasers provides ways to exercise and develop brain power! Each page stands alone and can be used as a quick and easy filler activity. The pages can be distributed to students as individual worksheets or made into transparencies for presentation to the entire class at once. The book is divided into sections so the teacher can find activities related to a subject being taught or to a particular student's needs. The activities are especially useful in helping students develop:

- Logic and other critical thinking skills.
- Creative thinking skills.
- Research skills.
- Spelling skills.
- General vocabulary skills.
- An understanding of the regionalized language of Western culture.

FAMOUS QUOTATIONS

Name the person responsible for each of these statements.

1. "All the world's a stage, and all the men and women merely players."

   _____

2. "I have not yet begun to fight." _____

3. "The only thing we have to fear is fear itself." _____

4. "Let them eat cake." _____

5. "I have a dream . . ." _____

6. "Give me liberty, or give me death!" _____

7. "That's one small step for a man, one giant leap for mankind."

   _____

8. "Two roads diverged in a wood, and I—I took the one less traveled by, and that has made all the difference." _____

9. "Ask not what your country can do for you—ask what you can do for your country." _____

10. "I never met a man I didn't like." _____

11. "You may fool all the people some of the time; you can even fool some of the people all the time; but you can't fool all of the people all the time." _____

12. "In this world nothing can be said to be certain, except death and taxes."

    _____

13. "The game isn't over till it's over." _____

14. "We hold these truths to be self-evident, that all men are created equal."

    _____

15. "The buck stops here." _____

INVENTORS AND THEIR INVENTIONS

Using items in the Invention Box below, write each invention next to the name of the person who is responsible for it.

1. Alexander Graham Bell _____

2. Elias Howe _____

3. Alfred B. Nobel _____

4. Eli Whitney _____

5. Clarence Birdseye _____

6. Henry Ford _____

7. Charles Goodyear _____

8. Thomas A. Edison _____

9. Guglielmo Marconi _____

10. Wright brothers _____

11. Johannes Gutenberg _____

12. John Deere _____

13. George M. Pullman _____

14. Benjamin Franklin _____

15. George Eastman _____

INVENTION BOX

dynamite • quick-freezing process of preserving food
steel plow • sewing machine • Kodak camera
electric light • wireless telegraph • bifocal glasses
vulcanization of rubber • first successful airplane
printing from movable type • telephone • railroad sleeping car
cotton gin • assembly line method of production

FAMOUS AMERICANS

Write the name of the person described in each phrase below.

1. The writer of "The Star-Spangled Banner." _____

2. The seamstress who is said to have made the first official U.S. flag.

   _____

3. The President of the Confederacy during the Civil War.

   _____

4. The founder of the American Red Cross. _____

5. The scientist who discovered more than 300 uses for peanuts.

   _____

6. The Sioux leader in the battle of the Little Bighorn in which General

   Custer died. _____

7. The pioneer who explored and settled Kentucky. _____

8. The skillful promoter who started the Barnum and Bailey Circus.

   _____

9. The pioneer who planted apple trees. _____

10. The advocate of women's suffrage who is pictured on the one-dollar

    coin. _____

11. The first black man to play major league baseball. _____

12. A Native American who played professional baseball and football and

    won Olympic gold medals in track and field. _____

13. The author of *Poor Richard's Almanac.* _____

14. The author of *Little Women* and *Little Men.* _____

15. The author of *The Sun Also Rises* and *The Old Man and the Sea.*

    _____

U.S. PRESIDENTS

1. Which President never lived in the White House? _____

2. Which President was sworn into office on an airplane?

    _____

3. Which President resigned from office? _____

4. Which President is pictured on the one-dollar bill? _____

5. Which President was nicknamed Ike? _____

6. Who was the only President to get married in the White House?

    _____

7. Which two Presidents were father and son? _____

    _____

8. Which President was born on the Fourth of July? _____

9. Who was our 22nd and 24th President? _____

10. Who was President during the Great Depression and WWII?

    _____

11. Which President also served as chief justice? _____

12. Which President weighed over 300 pounds? _____

13. Which President had the most children? _____

14. Which President served the shortest time in office? _____

15. Which President summed up his policy by saying, "Speak softly, and
    carry a big stick"? _____

16. Who was President during the Civil War? _____

17. Which President was nicknamed Old Rough and Ready?

    _____

18. Which President arranged the Louisiana Purchase? _____

FAMOUS FIRSTS

Write the names that correctly answer the following questions.
Who was the first . . .

1. American in space? _____

2. American woman in space? _____

3. American to orbit Earth? _____

4. American to walk in space? _____

5. Person to walk on the moon? _____

6. President of the U.S.? _____

7. Vice President of the U.S.? _____

8. Woman to run for President of the U.S.? _____

9. Republican President of the U.S.? _____

10. Woman to run for Vice President on the Democratic ticket?

    _____

11. English child born in America? _____

12. Signer of the Declaration of Independence? _____

13. Black soloist to sing with the Metropolitan Opera of New York City?

    _____

14. Woman in the U.S. to receive a medical degree?

    _____

15. Pilot to fly an aircraft faster than the speed of sound?

    _____

CONTINENT MATCH

List the countries in the Country Box under the appropriate continent.

AFRICA

_____
_____
_____
_____
_____
_____
_____
_____
_____
_____

ASIA

_____
_____
_____
_____
_____
_____
_____
_____
_____
_____

EUROPE

_____
_____
_____
_____
_____
_____
_____
_____
_____
_____

NORTH AMERICA

_____
_____
_____
_____
_____
_____
_____
_____
_____
_____

SOUTH AMERICA

_____
_____
_____
_____
_____
_____
_____
_____
_____

COUNTRY BOX
Switzerland, Kenya, Costa Rica, Canada, Saudi Arabia, Libya, United Kingdom, Brazil, Venezuela, Iran, Japan, Spain, Israel, France, Nicaragua, Ethiopia, Vietnam, Poland, Chile, Nigeria, El Salvador, Ecuador, Thailand, Cuba, Morocco, Iraq, United States, Sweden, Algeria, Egypt, China, Germany, Uruguay, Philippines, Guatemala, Italy, India, Bolivia, Angola, Greece, Mexico, Sudan, Colombia, Peru, Panama, Paraguay, Greenland, Tanzania, Hungary, Argentina

NAME THE COUNTRIES

Name the countries in which you would find the following cities and geographical features.

1. Toronto, Rocky Mountains, Hudson Bay, Victoria Island _____

2. River Shannon, Dublin, Wicklow Mountains, Limerick _____

3. Ganges River, New Delhi, Calcutta, Deccan Plateau _____

4. Nile River, Cairo, Mount Sinai, Suez Canal _____

5. Osaka, Mount Fuji, Hiroshima, Suo Sea _____

6. Amazon River, Rio de Janeiro, rain forest, Salvador _____

7. Hamburg, Danube River, Bonn, Black Forest _____

8. Yangtze River, Kunlun Mountains, Beijing, Shanghai _____

9. Lake Vanern, Dal River, Norrkoping, Stockholm _____

10. Loire River, Alps, Marseille, Paris _____

11. Baja California, Acapulco, Rio Grande, Mazatlan _____

12. Madrid, Iberian Mountains, Barcelona, Jucar River _____

13. Great Victoria Desert, Melbourne, Murray River, Sydney _____

14. Cape Town, Vaal River, Johannesburg, Drakensberg Mountains _____

15. Casablanca, Tangier, Atlas Mountains, Rabat _____

16. Buenos Aires, Pampas, Parana River, Cordoba _____

17. Thames River, London, Liverpool, Edinburgh _____

18. Naples, Sicily, Rome, Mount Vesuvius _____

19. St. Petersburg, Moscow, Ural Mountains, Siberia _____

20. Alps, Innsbruck, Vienna, Danube River _____

LANDMARKS

Using the places listed in the Places Box, identify where each landmark is located.

1. Big Ben _____

2. Colosseum _____

3. Eiffel Tower _____

4. Golden Gate Bridge _____

5. Great Pyramid _____

6. Taj Mahal _____

7. Gateway Arch _____

8. Parthenon _____

9. Empire State Building _____

10. Great Wall _____

11. Space Needle _____

12. Tivoli Gardens _____

13. Chichén Itzá _____

14. Kremlin _____

15. Astrodome _____

PLACES BOX

Denmark   India   New York City   Moscow   Seattle

London   Athens   Egypt   Rome   St. Louis

China   Houston   San Francisco   Paris   Mexico

STATE CAPITALS

Write the capitals of all 50 states in the puzzle according to the clues below.

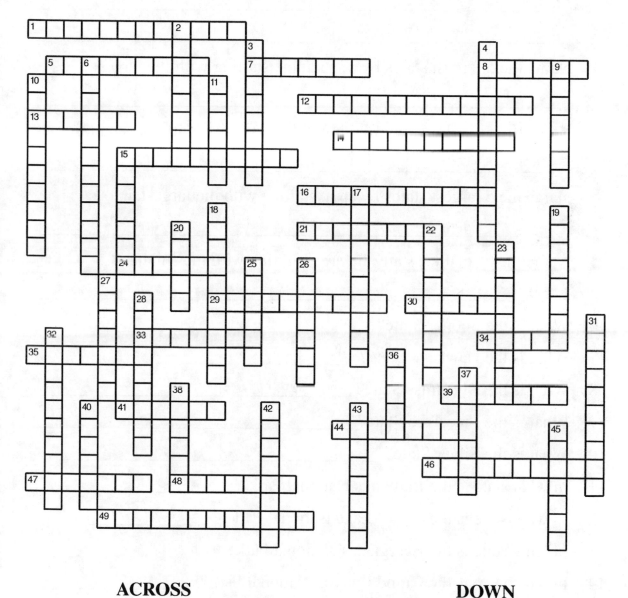

ACROSS				DOWN		
1. OK	16. FL	39. MI		2. OH	18. CA	31. VT
5. TN	21. CT	41. MA		3. SC	19. WY	32. PA
7. WA	24. CO	44. ND		4. IL	20. DE	36. OR
8. SD	29. AL	46. RI		6. UT	22. IA	37. MS
12. MO	30. KS	47. NJ		9. NC	23. MD	38. MN
13. TX	33. GA	48. NE		10. WV	25. AK	40. MT
14. LA	34. ID	49. IN		11. NY	26. AZ	42. HI
15. NV	35. WI			15. NH	27. ME	43. VA
				17. AR	28. KY	45. NM

U.S. CITIES, STATES, AND PARKS

1. Name the 10 largest cities in the U.S., starting with the largest.

_____

_____

2. Name the 5 largest states by population, starting with the largest.

_____

3. Name the 5 smallest states by population, starting with the smallest.

_____

4. Name the 5 largest states by area, starting with the largest.

_____

5. Name the 5 smallest states by area, starting with the smallest.

_____

6. What is the Sooner State? _____

7. What is the Hawkeye State? _____

8. What is the Bluegrass State? _____

9. What is the Pine Tree State? _____

10. What is the Silver State? _____

11. In what state is the Badlands National Park? _____

12. In what state is the Crater Lake National Park? _____

13. In what state is the Everglades National Park? _____

14. In what state is the Grand Canyon National Park? _____

15. In what state is the Yosemite National Park? _____

Bonus Questions: Name the northernmost U.S. city. _____

Name the southernmost U.S. city. _____

Name the easternmost U.S. city. _____

Name the westernmost U.S. city. _____

SPECIFIC GROUPS

Explain what the items in each list below have in common. Be specific.
An example has been done for you.

Football, baseball, soccer, hockey — team sports

1. Orioles, Royals, Rangers, Yankees _____

2. Bears, Cowboys, Vikings, Rams _____

3. Beets, carrots, turnips, potatoes _____

4. Lime, lemon, orange, grapefruit _____

5. Plum, peach, pear, pineapple _____

6. September, April, June, November _____

7. Snickers™, PayDay™, Almond Joy™ _____

8. Tiger, lion, panther, jaguar _____

9. Dragons, unicorns, mermaids _____

10. Bicycle, train, car, bus _____

11. Lincoln, Grant, Coolidge, Reagan _____

12. Cleveland, FDR, Kennedy, Carter _____

13. Texas, Louisiana, Mississippi, Alabama, Florida

    _____

14. Maine, Massachusetts, New Jersey, Virginia, South Carolina, Florida

    _____

15. California, Arizona, New Mexico, Texas

    _____

Bonus Question: Iowa, Missouri, Arkansas

    _____

WHICH ONE DOESN'T BELONG?

In each list below, circle the item that doesn't belong and explain what the other items have in common.

1. Delicious, Jonathan, McIntosh, Winesap, Bartlett, Granny Smith

   _____

2. Boy, lad, niece, man, husband, father, uncle, nephew, grandfather, son

   _____

3. Almanac, dictionary, math, atlas, encyclopedia, thesaurus

   _____

4. Iris, petunia, violet, daffodil, tulip, maple, rose, daisy, orchid, lily

   _____

5. Chicken, pig, cow, horse, goat, sheep, zebra, giraffe, cat, dog, tiger

   _____

6. Pen, pencil, crayon, chalk, eraser, marker, colored pencils

   _____

7. Red, yellow, blue, green

   _____

8. Dalmatian, cocker spaniel, dachshund, schnauzer, pug, angora

   _____

9. Cirrus, cumulus, stratus, calculus, altocumulus, cirrostratus

   _____

10. Kilometer, acre, gram, centimeter, milliliter, hectogram, deciliter

   _____

Bonus Question: Circle, square, triangle, rectangle, sphere, octagon

   _____

ANIMAL FAMILIES AND GROUPS

Fill in the blanks in the chart.

ANIMAL	MALE	FEMALE	YOUNG	GROUP
cattle	_____	cow	_____	_____
sheep	ram	_____	_____	_____
seal	bull	_____	pup	herd
kangaroo	_____	doe	_____	herd
hog	_____	_____	piglet	herd
lion	lion	lioness	_____	_____
ostrich	cock	hen	_____	_____
whale	_____	_____	calf	herd
chicken	rooster	_____	_____	_____
goat	_____	nanny	_____	herd
goose	_____	goose	_____	_____
fox	dog	_____	cub	skulk

WORD TWINS

Write the other half of each phrase below.

1. Cup and _____

2. Back and _____

3. Up and _____

4. Safe and _____

5. Nuts and _____

6. Thick and _____

7. Knife and _____

8. Pork and _____

9. Yes and _____

10. Read and _____

11. Lost and _____

12. Aches and _____

13. Soap and _____

14. Stop and _____

15. Live and _____

16. Salt and _____

17. Sticks and _____

18. Toss and _____

19. High and _____

20. Now and _____

21. Good and _____

22. Right and _____

23. Left and _____

24. Sing and _____

25. Look and _____

26. Black and _____

27. Come and _____

28. Pins and _____

29. Tooth and _____

30. Touch and _____

31. Bacon and _____

32. Macaroni and _____

33. Bread and _____

34. Meat and _____

35. Liver and _____

36. Potatoes and _____

37. Pride and _____

38. Prim and _____

39. Hand and _____

40. Hammer and _____

FAMILY VACATION

The McNeil family spent five days of their vacation in Florida. They visited a different tourist attraction each day. Using the clues below, determine which day they visited each attraction.

	Tues.	Wed.	Thurs.	Fri.	Sat.
Walt Disney World				yes	
Sea World	yes				
EPCOT Center					yes
Universal Studios Florida		yes			
Orlando Science Center			yes		

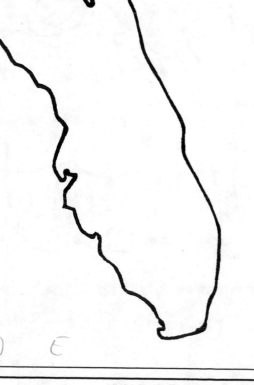

Clue 1: The McNeil family decided to go to Sea World before they went to Universal Studios Florida.

Clue 2: They decided to go to EPCOT Center the day after visiting Walt Disney World.

Clue 3: They went to Walt Disney World two days after visiting Universal Studios Florida.

THUNDERSTORM CONFUSION

In the confusion of the thunderstorm, the animals got out of their stalls. Using the clues below, help Michael get them back into their proper stalls.

Clue 1: The pig and cow are in stalls at opposite ends of the barn.

Clue 2: The horse belongs in the third stall.

Clue 3: The goat is in the stall between the pig and sheep.

Clue 4: The temporary home for the rabbits is in the remaining stall.

1   2   3   4   5   6

____   ____   ____   ____   ____   ____

BASEBALL BATTING ORDER

Use the following clues to line up Coach Shaffer's team in the correct batting order. Amos is one of the players.

Clue 1: Phil is before Henrik, who is 7th to bat.

Clue 2: Alex and Bill are the first and last batters, in no particular order.

Clue 3: There are 4 batters after Emilio.

Clue 4: Bill did not get to bat in the first inning.

Clue 5: In the second inning, Emilio hit a triple, which allowed Jakob to score.

Clue 6: Dan is hitting between Todd and Alex.

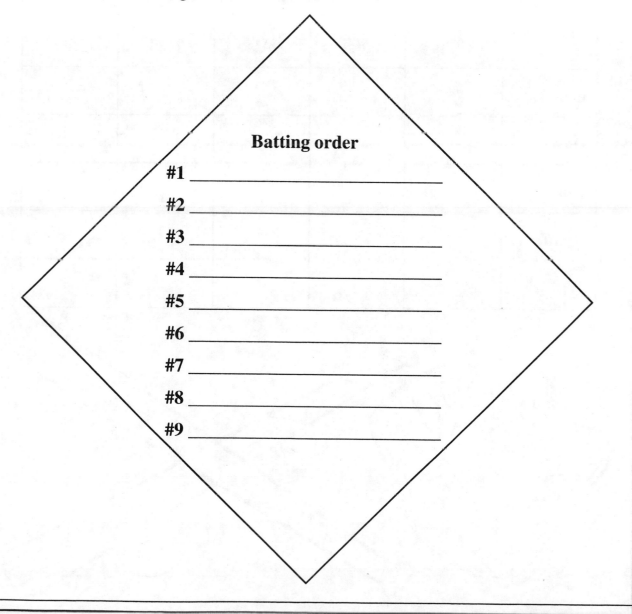

Batting order

#1 _____

#2 _____

#3 _____

#4 _____

#5 _____

#6 _____

#7 _____

#8 _____

#9 _____

FAVORITE TEAMS

Five boys like different baseball teams. Read the clues to determine which team each likes best.

Clue 1: No boy's favorite team begins with the same letter as his name.

Clue 2: Chad and Ryan like the Dodgers, the Reds, or the A's.

Clue 3: Will's bedroom is filled with A's posters and products.

Clue 4: Adam's father is a big Cubs fan, but Adam is not.

	Cubs	Dodgers	A's	Reds	White Sox
Chad					
Dave					
Adam					
Ryan					
Will					

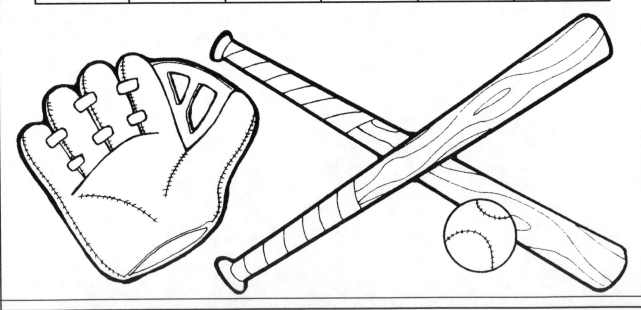

GET TO KNOW YOUR CLASSMATES

**Fill each blank with the name of a classmate who fits the description.
Use each person's name only once. Don't forget to include yourself!**

1. Has an unusual pet   _____

2. Was born outside the state   _____

3. Has seen a rainbow   _____

4. Loves country music   _____

5. Has red hair   _____

6. Lives or has lived on a farm   _____

7. Is a Chicago Bears fan   _____

8. Loves strawberry milkshakes   _____

9. Has purple as a favorite color   _____

10. Loves to go camping   _____

11. Has no cavities   _____

12. Hates liver   _____

13. Has a middle name identical to yours   _____

14. Is left-handed   _____

15. Has 7 as a favorite number   _____

16. Has milked a cow   _____

17. Has been to a museum   _____

18. Has met a famous person   _____

19. Has blue eyes   _____

20. Has math as a favorite subject   _____

WHAT'S THE QUESTION?

Write a question for each of the following answers.

1. _____

   Apple pie.

2. _____

   A tornado.

3. _____

   Mars.

4. _____

   100.

5. _____

   In the year 2002.

6. _____

   Napoleon.

7. _____

   Leonardo da Vinci.

8. _____

   Frank Lloyd Wright.

9. _____

   Yes!

10. _____

    No!

11. _____

    13.

12. _____

    The Kentucky Derby.

22

ART, MUSIC, LITERATURE

Find an item in either the Art Box, Music Box, or Literature Box that relates to each clue below.

1. Leonardo da Vinci _____

2. Michelangelo _____

3. Claude Monet _____

4. Grant Wood _____

5. Ansel Adams _____

6. Rock _____

7. Jazz _____

8. Ballet _____

9. Opera _____

10. *Moonlight Sonata* _____

11. *The Best of Simple* _____

12. *Pride and Prejudice* _____

13. *A Christmas Carol* _____

14. "The Raven" _____

15. *The Adventures of Huckleberry Finn* _____

ART BOX	MUSIC BOX	LITERATURE BOX
photography	Beethoven	Charles Dickens
impressionism	*The Nutcracker*	Mark Twain
Sistine Chapel	Duke Ellington	Jane Austen
Mona Lisa	*Aida*	Langston Hughes
American Gothic	Beatles	Edgar Allan Poe

HIDDEN MEANINGS

Explain the meaning of each box.

K C E H C	**GOING** DIET	**TIME** A B D E
1. _____	2. _____	3. _____
man ――――― *board*	B R A I N E D	cycle cycle cycle
4. _____	5. _____	6. _____
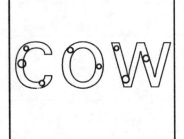	**GI** ――― **CCC**	H IJKLMN O
7. _____	8. _____	9. _____
1,00 **1** 0,000	T O U C H	DECI SION
10. _____	11. _____	12. _____

MORE HIDDEN MEANINGS

Explain the meaning of each box.

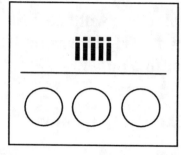

1. _____

M	E
A	L

2. _____

TI*JUST*ME

3. _____

HOUR

4. _____

MAC

5. _____

GROUND
FT   FT
FT   FT
FT   FT

6. _____

ban   ana

7. _____

MO_{MAN}ON

8. _____

wear
―――――
long

9. _____

1

10. _____

B.A.
M.A.
PhD.
―――――
0

11. _____

L A

12. _____

CHANGE FOR A DOLLAR

There are over 100 ways to make change for a dollar. Work with a friend and list as many ways as you can. List the coins in order on each line, from largest to smallest. (Hint: Working from large to small coins will help you find more ways to make change, too.) The list has been started for you. If you need more space, continue your list on the back of this paper.

Use the following abbreviations:
hd (half dollar)   q (quarter)   d (dime)   n (nickel)   p (penny)

1. 2 hd
2. 1 hd, 2 q
3. 1 hd, 5 d
4. 1 hd, 10 n
5. _____
6. _____
7. _____
8. _____
9. _____
10. _____
11. _____
12. _____
13. _____
14. _____
15. _____
16. _____
17. _____
18. _____
19. _____
20. _____

21. _____
22. _____
23. _____
24. _____
25. _____
26. _____
27. _____
28. _____
29. _____
30. _____
31. _____
32. _____
33. _____
34. _____
35. _____
36. _____
37. _____
38. _____
39. _____
40. _____

41. _____
42. _____
43. _____
44. _____
45. _____
46. _____
47. _____
48. _____
49. _____
50. _____
51. _____
52. _____
53. _____
54. _____
55. _____
56. _____
57. _____
58. _____
59. _____
60. _____

ADD AND SUBTRACT

Place + and - signs between the digits so that both sides of each equation are equal.

1.   3   5   3   9   6   5   4   2   =   13

2.   9   8   1   2   9   6   8   8   =   5

3.   1   6   3   7   9   4   5   7   =   16

4.   6   3   2   8   5   7   4   6   =   17

5.   2   1   8   9   4   9   7   2   =   10

6.   5   8   2   7   3   6   2   9   =   6

7.   5   3   5   4   4   2   9   8   =   10

8.   7   6   2   9   9   3   7   2   =   17

9.   6   3   8   3   2   5   2   9   =   6

10.   4   9   6   5   2   8   4   1   =   7

NUMBERS, NUMBERS, NUMBERS

Answer each question with a number. How many . . .

1. Oceans are on Earth? _____

2. Sides does a pentagon have? _____

3. Planets are in our solar system? _____

4. Suns are in our solar system? _____

5. Teeth does an adult have? _____

6. Parts of speech are there? _____

7. Eyes did Cyclops have? _____

8. Degrees are in a right angle? _____

9. Lakes are in the Great Lakes? _____

10. Notes are in an octave? _____

11. Countries are in the continent of Australia? _____

12. Teaspoons are in a tablespoon? _____

13. Atoms are in a water molecule? _____

14. Amendments are in the Bill of Rights? _____

15. Verses are in "The Star-Spangled Banner"? _____

16. Cells are in an amoeba? _____

17. Tablespoons are in a cup? _____

18. Stories are there in the Sears Tower? _____

19. Faces are carved in Mount Rushmore? _____

20. Musical instruments are played in an a cappella performance? _____

CALCULATOR SPELLING

Perform each math problem on your calculator. Then turn your calculator upside-down to find an answer for each of the following clues.

1. Santa's laughter — $0.20202 + 0.20202$ — _____

2. Not tight — $50,000 - 14,993$ — _____

3. Synonym for cry — $457 + 275 + 73$ — _____

4. Petroleum — $413 + 216 + 81$ — _____

5. Garden tool used to water plants — $2,106 + 1,398$ — _____

6. More or _____ — $7,836 - 2,299$ — _____

7. Foot apparel — $956 + 125 + 486 + 1,478$ — _____

8. Antonym for little — $1,000 - 255 - 127$ — _____

9. 212° F. — $6,188 - 2,356 + 5,189 - 1,913$ — _____

10. Synonym for dirt — $1,456 + 6,112 - 2,589 + 2,126$ — _____

11. To ask earnestly — $780 - 89 - 53$ — _____

12. A man's name — $147 + 369 + 205 + 87$ — _____

13. _____, fight, win — $.3 + .3$ — _____

14. An empty space — $688 + 1,482 + 1,534$ — _____

15. To laugh in a silly way — $188,308 + 188,308$ — _____

EQUATIONS

Each equation below contains the initials of words that will make it complete. Find the missing words. An example has been done for you.

36 = I in a Y   36 inches in a yard

1. 3 = V in a T _____

2. 4 = Q in a G _____

3. 6 = S of a H _____

4. 11 = P on a F T _____

5. 12 = E in a D _____

6. 12 = I in a F _____

7. 16 = O in a P _____

8. 20 = Y in a S _____

9. 52 = C in a D _____

10. 60 = S in a M _____

11. 60 = M in an H _____

12. 64 = S on a C _____

13. 100 = Y in a C _____

14. 100 = P in a D _____

15. 144 = I in a G _____

16. 360 = D in a C _____

17. 366 = D in a L Y _____

18. 1000 = M in a M _____

19. 2000 = P in a T _____

20. 5280 = F in a M _____

TRIVIA TIME

1. Whose portrait appears on the ten dollar bill? _____

2. Which is nearer, the moon or the sun? _____

3. How many numbers are in a zip code? _____

4. In bowling, how many pins are in the back row? _____

5. Which is more, minimum or maximum? _____

6. To indicate a left turn, which way do you push the car's turning signal lever, up or down? _____

7. In a fraction, what is the top number called? _____

8. Are there more red or white stripes on the U.S. flag? _____

9. In what sport do teams compete for the Davis Cup? _____

10. What is the first book in the Bible? _____

11. In which hand does the Statue of Liberty hold a tablet? _____

12. From the sun, what is the sixth planet? _____

13. How many dots are on a pair of dice? _____

14. How many spaces are on a checkerboard? _____

15. When traveling north, what direction is to the left? _____

16. What title is given to a queen's daughter? _____

17. What color are traffic lights, from top to bottom? _____

18. What is the last car on a freight train called? _____

19. On what part of your body would you wear a monocle? _____

20. Of what are pennies made? _____

SCIENCE TRIVIA

1. What is another name for low clouds? _____

2. What do we call an instrument that makes small things look larger?

    _____

3. What is the largest planet in our solar system? _____

4. What is the device used to measure air pressure? _____

5. What is a frog called when it still has gills? _____

6. What is the hardest natural substance known? _____

7. What do we call the dirty haze that forms when air pollution combines

    with moisture in the air? _____

8. What animal uses its smell as a weapon? _____

9. What makes our skeleton move? _____

10. How many legs does a spider have? _____

11. Which bones protect your lungs and heart? _____

12. For most people, what is the normal body temperature? _____

13. Which is larger, the moon or Earth? _____

14. What bird can fly backward? _____

15. What part of the body is sometimes called the "funny bone"?

    _____

16. What kind of trees lose their leaves in the autumn? _____

17. What substance gives plants their green color? _____

18. What system of the human body is made up of blood, blood vessels,

    and the heart? _____

19. What is the colored part of the eye called? _____

20. What is a general term for computer programs? _____

U.S. TRIVIA

1. Who is said to have discovered America in 1492? _____

2. Who assassinated President Abraham Lincoln? _____

3. What was the last state to join the United States? _____

4. What is the U.S. flag's nickname? _____

5. What document was signed on July 4, 1776? _____

6. What is the motto of the United States? _____

7. How did Davy Crockett die? _____

8. At the end of the Civil War, who was the Southern general who surrendered? _____

9. To what Northern general did he surrender? _____

10. What game is played every January to determine the championship of the National Football League? _____

11. During what war did the Battle of Bunker Hill take place?

    _____

12. With what war was the Mason-Dixon line associated? _____

13. What was William Cody's nickname? _____

14. What sport did Babe Ruth play? _____

15. With what organization was Edgar J. Hoover associated? _____

16. When was D-Day? _____

17. The phrase "the shot heard round the world" refers to what war?

    _____

18. Which President was associated with Watergate? _____

19. Which document begins with the words, "We, the people?"

    _____

20. What is NASA? _____

WHICH IS IT?

Circle the right answer.

1.	Dozen	6	12	13
2.	Rectangle	4 sides	5 sides	6 sides
3.	State	Denver	England	Utah
4.	Thomas Jefferson	3rd President	16th President	40th President
5.	United States	13 states	48 states	50 states
6.	U.S. capital	Chicago	L.A.	Washington, D.C.
7.	Year	12 months	50 weeks	360 days
8.	Day	12 hours	24 hours	60 minutes
9.	Decade	10 years	20 years	100 years
10.	Rooms in the White House	75	132	210
11.	Dodecagon	10 sides	12 sides	15 sides
12.	Baker's dozen	12	13	15
13.	Muscles in the body	over 200	over 400	over 600
14.	Thanksgiving	September	November	December
15.	Capital of Texas	Austin	Dallas	Houston
16.	16th President	Jefferson	Lincoln	Washington
17.	Cloud formation	calculus	cumulus	omnibus
18.	Peninsula	Florida	Hawaii	Wyoming
19.	Percussion instrument	tambourine	trombone	violin
20.	Painter	Bach	Beethoven	Picasso

THE LARGEST TO THE SMALLEST

What is the . . .

1. Largest island? _____

2. Smallest breed of dog? _____

3. Largest freshwater lake? _____

4. Longest mountain range? _____

5. Smallest continent? _____

6. Largest snake? _____

7. Largest sea? _____

8. Largest country? _____

9. Highest mountain peak? _____

10. Largest animal? _____

11. Largest ocean? _____

12. Longest river? _____

13. Largest desert? _____

14. Fastest animal on land? _____

15. Smallest bird? _____

ACRONYMS

Acronyms are words formed from the initial letters of other words. An example is TGIF which means "thank goodness it's Friday." What do the following acronyms mean?

1. VIP _____

2. IRS _____

3. TLC _____

4. KO _____

5. COD _____

6. POW _____

7. DA _____

8. DJ _____

9. MIA _____

10. AARP _____

11. NATO _____

12. IQ _____

13. VDT _____

14. UNESCO _____

15. SPCA _____

Bonus Questions:

RSVP _____

FIFO _____

ANTONYMS, HOMOPHONES, SYNONYMS

Identify each pair of words as antonyms, homophones, or synonyms.

1. ate / eight _____

2. problem / solution _____

3. ally / friend _____

4. following / preceding _____

5. attempt / endeavor _____

6. vast / minute _____

7. accept / except _____

8. sufficient / ample _____

9. foe / opposition _____

10. gorgeous / beautiful _____

11. praise / preys _____

12. desire / crave _____

13. individual / group _____

14. stationary / stationery _____

15. difficult / troublesome _____

16. allowed / aloud _____

17. different / unique _____

18. something / nothing _____

19. repeatedly / frequently _____

20. together / apart _____

IF AND WHERE TO USE THE HYPHEN

Rewrite the words below, inserting hyphens or spaces if and where they are needed.

1. jacko'lantern _____

2. nontransferable _____

3. autobiography _____

4. brotherinlaw _____

5. onceover _____

6. undergraduate _____

7. attorneygeneral _____

8. oldfashioned _____

9. lefthanded _____

10. allready _____

11. hideandseek _____

12. weatherbureau _____

13. twothirds _____

14. coauthor _____

15. knowitall _____

16. thirtynine _____

17. outofdate _____

18. openended _____

19. twobyfour _____

20. ongoing _____

SHORT FORM/LONG FORM

The following words are written in their "short form." Write the "long form" of these words in the blanks on the right. In the blanks at the bottom of the page, write both the "short form" and "long form" of five more words.

	Short Form	**Long Form**
1.	gas	_____
2.	math	_____
3.	limo	_____
4.	doc	_____
5.	fridge	_____
6.	burger	_____
7.	plane	_____
8.	lab	_____
9.	auto	_____
10.	exam	_____
11.	ref	_____
12.	champ	_____
13.	grad	_____
14.	sub	_____
15.	phone	_____
16.	_____	_____
17.	_____	_____
18.	_____	_____
19.	_____	_____
20.	_____	_____

RHYMING WORD PAIRS

Find an adjective that rhymes with a noun so that together, the two words have about the same meaning as the phrase that is given. An example has been done for you.

comical rabbit   funny bunny

1. Bashful insect   _____

2. Burned bread   _____

3. Unhappy friend   _____

4. Obese feline   _____

5. Minor car crash   _____

6. Colorless man   _____

7. Large swine   _____

8. Ill hen   _____

9. Overweight rodent   _____

10. Fine orchestra   _____

11. Little snack   _____

12. Enjoyable jogging   _____

13. Soaked dog   _____

14. Bloody tale   _____

15. Twice as much bother   _____

16. Ailing creepy crawler _____

17. Light red beverage   _____

18. Tiny bug   _____

19. Clever feline   _____

20. Dejected boy   _____

WHICH WORD?

Words that sound alike or look alike often have meanings that are not alike at all! Decide which word is the correct one and circle it.

1. A result   affect / effect
2. A heavenly body   angel / angle
3. Second in a series of two   later / latter
4. To take that which is offered   accept / except
5. To stop   quiet / quit / quite
6. In any case   any way / anyway
7. Unlawful   elicit / illicit
8. Writing paper   stationary / stationery
9. Complete   thorough / through
10. To go forward   precede / proceed
11. To prove something is false   disapprove / disprove
12. A part of speech   preposition / proposition
13. To hint or suggest   imply / infer
14. Lansing, Michigan   capital / capitol
15. Dry land   desert / dessert

WORD CHAIN

Use the last two letters of the first word in the word chain to begin the next word. Continue throughout the chain.

Thin mist   haze

1. Animal covered by black and white stripes   _____

2. Plant used to make furniture   _____

3. To reply to   _____

4. To rub out   _____

5. More than two but not many   _____

6. State whose capital is Montgomery   _____

7. Pasta formed into tubes   _____

8. A sister's daughter   _____

9. Wormlike animal with many pairs of legs   _____

10. To refuse   _____

11. Antonym of positive   _____

12. Stanza of a poem or hymn   _____

13. To close securely   _____

14. Narrow lane between buildings   _____

15. Organ of sight   _____

16. Twelve months   _____

17. The designing of buildings   _____

18. Directions for cooking a dish   _____

19. Person who is walking   _____

20. Troubled and worried   _____

Unable to produce good results   useless

COMPETITIVE WORD CHAIN

Two or more players start at the same time. The object is to fill in all the blanks with a 3-, 4-, 5-, or 6-letter word, depending on the number of blanks given. Each word must begin with the last letter of the preceding word. The first word may start with any letter. (Words may not be repeated.) The first player to complete all the words wins.

1. _ _ _
2. _ _ _ _
3. _ _ _ _ _
4. _ _ _ _ _ _
5. _ _ _ _ _
6. _ _ _ _
7. _ _ _
8. _ _ _ _
9. _ _ _ _ _
10. _ _ _ _ _ _
11. _ _ _ _ _
12. _ _ _ _
13. _ _ _
14. _ _ _ _
15. _ _ _ _ _
16. _ _ _ _ _ _
17. _ _ _ _ _
18. _ _ _ _
19. _ _ _

WORD WINDERS

Use the clues to help you fill in the blanks and circles. Only the circled letters change from one word to the next.

	A fish that can be dangerous	s	h	a	r	k
1.	Pointed	_	_	_	_	◯
2.	To use together	_	_	_	_	◯
3.	To be concerned	◯	_	_	_	_
4.	A horse-drawn vehicle with two wheels	_	_	_	_	◯
5.	A navigator's map	◯	◯	_	_	_
6.	To delight	_	_	_	_	◯
7.	Not soft	_	_	_	◯	_
8.	A rabbit	_	_	_	_	◯
9.	Money paid to ride a bus	_	◯	_	_	_
10.	Land used to raise crops	_	_	_	◯	_
11.	A signal used to give warning	◯	◯	_	_	_
12.	A small songbird	_	_	_	_	◯
13.	The sound a dog makes	_	◯	_	_	_
14.	Without light	_	◯	_	_	_
15.	To have sufficient courage	_	_	_	_	◯
16.	A fruit	_	_	◯	_	_
17.	After the usual time	_	◯	_	_	_
18.	A bowling alley	_	_	◯	_	_
19.	A walking stick	_	◯	_	_	_
20.	A wafer for holding ice cream	_	◯	_	_	_
	Finished		d	o	n	e

ONE WORD PLUS ANOTHER

Add one word to another word to make a third word.

1. To decay _____

    and the past tense of eat _____

    make a word meaning to revolve _____.

2. To put on _____

    and something that provides access or insight _____

    make a member of the horse family _____.

3. A standard score for a hole of golf _____

    plus to get possession of _____

    make a word meaning to participate _____.

4. An auto _____

    plus an animal that is treated with affection _____

    make a type of floor covering _____.

5. A flower that is not fully open _____

    plus to obtain _____

    make a plan of income and expenses _____.

6. A lower limb of the human body _____

    plus the antonym for begin _____

    make a story handed down from the past _____.

7. To succeed in competition _____

    and an endeavor _____

    make a word meaning cold _____.

8. A kind of tree _____

    plus a rock from which metal can be extracted _____

    make a word meaning on land _____.

LETTER ANSWERS

Use one or two letters of the alphabet to answer each of the clues.

A B C D E G H

Z

1. Not difficult   _____

2. Body of water   _____

3. An exclamation   _____

4. An insect   _____

5. Something to drink   _____

6. A vegetable   _____

7. A question   _____

8. A girl's name   _____

9. A plant or vine   _____

10. Native American home   _____

11. Good-by   _____

12. Body part used for sight   _____

13. Radio announcer   _____

14. Cold   _____

15. A pronoun   _____

 Y X W V

I J K L M

U T S R Q P O N

COLORFUL WORDS

Answer each clue with a word that has the name of a color in it.

1. A contagious disease _____

2. A famous pirate _____

3. A fruit _____

4. A medal _____

5. A person without training or experience _____

6. Beef, veal, pork, and lamb _____

7. A bird _____

8. An automobile tire _____

9. A vegetable _____

10. A piece of slate on which to write with chalk _____

11. A flower _____

12. A bus line _____

13. A chocolate cookie-like cake _____

14. A wasp _____

15. A bridge in California _____

RE"CON"STRUCT THESE WORDS

Each phrase below is a clue for an answer that contains the letters
c o n.

1. To hide   c o n _ _ _ _

2. The seven main land masses on Earth   c o n _ _ _ _ _ _ _

3. To make friends again; to make agree   _ _ c o n _ _ _ _

4. A musical entertainment   c o n _ _ _ _

5. Letters that are not vowels   c o n _ _ _ _ _ _

6. Seasonings for food   c o n _ _ _ _ _ _

7. The end   c o n _ _ _ _ _ _

8. To make up or fabricate   c o n _ _ _ _

9. Arguments for and against something   _ _ _ _ _ _ _ c o n _

10. Mixed up   c o n _ _ _ _ _

11. To extend good wishes to   c o n _ _ _ _ _ _ _ _ _ _

12. To go on   c o n _ _ _ _ _

13. Strong building material   c o n _ _ _ _ _

14. State whose capital is Hartford   C o n _ _ _ _ _ _ _

15. Bits of colored paper thrown at   c o n _ _ _ _ _
    celebrations

ARE YOU A WORD "FAN"?

Each phrase below is a clue for an answer that contains the letters
f a n.

1. Foot soldiers   _ _ f a n _ _ _

2. A soft, warm cloth of wool or cotton   f _ a n _ _ _

3. Enthusiastic beyond reason   f a n _ _ _ _

4. The threadlike wire that gives off
   light in an electric light bulb.   f _ _ a _ _ n _

5. Letters sent to celebrities   f a n   _ _ _ _

6. Strange; fabulous; unreal   f a n _ _ _ _ _ _

7. A showy display   f a n _ _ _ _

8. The power to imagine   f a n _ _

9. A pigeon whose tail spreads out   f a n _ _ _ _

10. Extreme scarcity of food   f a _ _ n _

11. Not committed in love   f a n _ _ - _ _ _ _

12. A product of the imagination   f a n _ _ _ _

13. A meteor   f a _ _ _ n _ _ _ _ _ _

14. A baby   _ _ f a n _

15. Long, pointed teeth of a snake   f a n _ _

NO! NO! A THOUSAND TIMES NO!

Each phrase below is a clue for an answer that contains the letters
n o.

1. Range of information   _ n o _ _ _ _ _ _

2. A loop with a slip knot that tightens as the rope is pulled   n o _ _ _

3. A lengthy story   n o _ _ _

4. Foolishness   n o _ _ _ _ _ _

5. Body part used for smelling   n o _ _

6. Small, odd-looking, imaginary being   _ n o _ _

7. A macaroni-like food made in flat strips   n o _ _ _ _

8. A wanderer   n o _ _ _

9. A pig's nose, mouth, and jaws   _ n o _ _

10. Either of the two times each year when day and night are of equal length   _ _ _ _ n o _

11. No one   n o _ _ _ _

12. A rap on the door   _ n o _ _

13. An unpleasant sound   n o _ _ _

14. The Biblical man who built an ark   N o _ _

15. A city in Tennessee   _ n o _ _ _ _ _

"CAR" PARTS OF WORDS

Each phrase below is a clue for an answer that contains the letters
c a r.

1. Saturday morning TV shows   c a r _ _ _ _ _
2. Major league team   C a r _ _ _ _ _ _
3. A box   c a r _ _ _
4. A sweater that opens down the front   c a r _ _ _ _ _
5. A floor covering   c a r _ _ _
6. Part of the engine of a car   c a r _ _ _ _ _ _ _
7. To get rid of   _ _ _ c a r _
8. A flower   c a r _ _ _ _ _ _
9. A traveling show   c a r _ _ _ _ _
10. A merry-go-round   c a r _ _ _ _ _
11. A picture that exaggerates a person's   c a r _ _ _ _ _ _ _
    peculiarities
12. To imprison   _ _ c a r _ _ _ _ _ _
13. Animals that feed chiefly on flesh   c a r _ _ _ _ _ _ _
14. A kind of candy   c a r _ _ _ _
15. Unit of weight for precious stones   c a r _ _

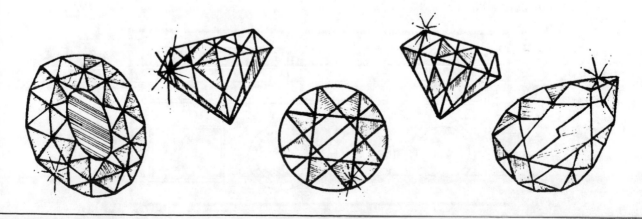

"THE" WORDS

Each phrase below is a clue for an answer that contains the letters
t h e.

1. Instrument used to measure temperature   t h e _ _ _ _ _ _ _
2. The act of stealing   t h e _ _
3. A place where movies are shown   t h e _ _ _ _
4. To wash; to immerse in liquid   _ _ t h e
5. A dictionary containing sets of words such as synonyms   t h e _ _ _ _ _ _
6. The study of numbers   _ _ t h e _ _ _ _ _ _
7. The atmospheric conditions of a place   _ _ _ t h e _
8. A black leopard   _ _ _ t h e _
9. Melody used to identify a certain show   t h e _ _   _ _ _ _
10. An essay submitted by a candidate for a university degree   t h e _ _ _
11. Near that place or time   t h e _ _ _ _ _ _ _ _
12. At that time   t h e _
13. An explanation; an opinion   t h e _ _ _
14. To bring together   _ _ t h e _
15. A device that regulates temperature automatically   t h e _ _ _ _ _ _ _

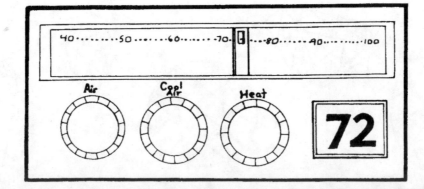

"BLACK" IS BEAUTIFUL

Each phrase below is a clue for an answer that contains the letters
b l a c k.

1. Surface material used on roads   b l a c k _ _ _

2. A vegetable   b l a c k - _ _ _ _   _ _ _

3. A fruit   b l a c k _ _ _ _ _

4. An attempt to obtain money by   b l a c k _ _ _ _
   threats

5. A spider   b l a c k   _ _ _ _ _

6. Discoloration caused by a bruise   b l a c k - _ _ _ - _ _ _ _

7. Petroleum; oil   b l a c k   _ _ _ _

8. A card game   b l a c k _ _ _ _

9. A collapsed object in space that has   b l a c k   _ _ _ _
   tremendously strong gravity

10. Illegal selling   b l a c k   _ _ _ _ _ _

11. The highest order in karate and judo   b l a c k _ _ _ _

12. A famous pirate   B l a c k _ _ _ _ _

13. Family member of whom others are   b l a c k   _ _ _ _ _
    ashamed

14. Mountains in South Dakota   B l a c k   _ _ _ _ _

15. A daisy   b l a c k - _ _ _ _   _ _ _ _ _

"CATS" AND "DOGS"

Each phrase below is a clue for an answer that contains either
c a t or d o g.

1. A booklet listing items for sale   c a t _ _ _ _

2. A swimming stroke   d o g _ _ _ _ _ _

3. A large church   c a t _ _ _ _ _ _

4. A soldier's ID   d o g _ _ _

5. A major disaster   c a t _ _ _ _ _ _ _

6. Exhausted, worn-out   d o g - _ _ _ _ _

7. Tall plants found in marshes   c a t _ _ _ _ _

8. A frankfurter   _ _ _ d o g

9. The larva of a butterfly   c a t _ _ _ _ _ _

10. One expected to lose   _ _ _ _ _ d o g

11. A quick snooze   c a t _ _ _

12. Having turned-down pages   d o g - _ _ _ _ _

13. A baseball player whose position is behind home plate   c a t _ _ _ _

14. A tree   d o g _ _ _ _

15. A boat with two hulls   c a t _ _ _ _ _ _

"HEADS" OR "TAILS"

Each phrase below is a clue for an answer that contains either
h e a d or t a i l.

1. An advantage at the start of a race   h e a d _ _ _ _ _

2. To drive dangerously close behind another vehicle   t a i l _ _ _ _

3. A descriptive title of a news story   h e a d _ _ _ _

4. One who makes clothes   t a i l _ _

5. A center of operations   h e a d _ _ _ _ _ _ _ _

6. The red rear light of a vehicle   t a i l _ _ _ _ _

7. Obstinate   h e a d _ _ _ _ _ _

8. The lowest or last part   t a i l _ _ _

9. Progress   h e a d _ _ _

10. An aircraft's spiral dive   t a i l _ _ _ _

11. A person in charge of a school   h e a d _ _ _ _ _ _

12. An offensive position in football   t a i l _ _ _ _

13. Thorough; complete   h e a d - _ _ - _ _ _

14. The part of a car that discharges the exhaust of the engine   t a i l _ _ _ _

15. A bright light on the front of a car   h e a d _ _ _ _ _

PUTTING THE PIECES TOGETHER

Choose one syllable from column A, one from B, and one from C to
form a three-syllable word. Write the new words in column D.
Use each syllable in each column only once.

Column A	Column B	Column C	Column D
mi	cle	ance	_____
car	o	struct	_____
re	low	ta	_____
dis	cro	sphere	_____
hem	pen	mate	_____
es	es	us	_____
nu	i	lel	_____
al	con	ter	_____
par	ti	wave	_____
fi	al	bey	_____

won	a	dy	_____
im	e	el	_____
un	li	ry	_____
trag	fi	ful	_____
live	or	ous	_____
bound	der	ize	_____
gov	rav	cial	_____
spe	ern	sive	_____
vig	cial	hood	_____
of	pres	ment	_____

WEATHER WORDS

Hidden in each sentence is a word that a meteorologist might use in a weather report. Each "weather word" can be found either in the middle of a word or by combining the end of one word with the beginning of the next. Underline the "weather word" in each sentence. An example has been done for you.

We found <u>mildew</u> around the pipes in the basement.

1. Do you like spicy foods?

2. My uncle drives a Thunderbird.

3. Heather is my best friend.

4. Wouldn't it be fun to sail the seas on a yacht?

5. Thomas is unlikely to win the race.

6. According to Cedric, loud is the only way to sing!

7. War might break out soon between those two countries.

8. Who could have torn a door from its hinges?

9. Be sure the sign is clearly visible from the road.

10. Steven sprained his ankle while riding his skateboard.

11. Mom had to scold Sarah for disobeying.

12. Nicklas went hunting and shot five ducks.

13. We'll have the show indoors this year.

14. Ha! Illness will never stop me!

15. Lindsay is now working at the mall.

CODED MESSAGE

Answer each question below. Then use the code to reveal a famous saying.

$\overline{}_{7}\ \overline{}_{2}\ \overline{}_{6}\quad \overline{}_{8}\ \overline{}_{5}\ \overline{}_{3}\quad \overline{}_{11}\ \overline{}_{1}\quad \overline{}_{7}\ \overline{}_{2}\ \overline{}_{6}$

$\overline{}_{9}\ \overline{}_{4}\ \overline{}_{11}\ \overline{}_{3}\ \overline{}_{10}\quad \overline{}_{7}\ \overline{}_{2}\ \overline{}_{6}\quad \overline{}_{8}\ \overline{}_{5}\ \overline{}_{3}.$

1. If a prairie dog is a dog, circle K. If it's a rodent, circle F.

2. If your mother's sister is your aunt, circle O. If not, circle A.

3. If 6 x 6 is 35, circle M. If not, circle N.

4. If antonyms are words that mean the opposite, circle H. If not, circle L.

5. If John F. Kennedy is one of the four famous faces carved on Mt. Rushmore, circle K. If not, circle A.

6. If the capital of Nevada is Reno, circle Y. If not, circle U.

7. If a trumpet is a woodwind instrument, circle Z. If not, circle Y.

8. If the Pilgrims landed on Plymouth Rock in 1492, circle S. If not, circle C.

9. If Charles Dickens wrote *David Copperfield*, circle T. If not, circle W.

10. If a telescope is used to view things far away, circle K. If not, circle M.

11. If the Louvre is located in London, circle E. If not, circle I.

DECODE AUTHORS AND ACTORS

Each group of letters below is a list of related names in code. Each group has its own code. Brainstorm some names to fit each category. Once you have identified a name, use the known letters to decode the other names.

Authors

1. FWHGRN   ENK   NFSWCC   _____

2. VNXR   SVPGRCGNX   NXZQPRQX   _____

3. AHZK   IFHEQ   _____

4. IQJQPFK   SFQNPK   _____

5. SVNPFQR   ZGSTQXR   _____

6. QEGFK   ZGSTGXRWX   _____

7. XNCVNXGQF   VNDCVWPXQ   _____

8. DGFFGNE   RVNTQRUQNPQ   _____

9. ENPT   CDNGX   _____

10. FNHPN   GXYNFFR   DGFZQP   _____

Actors

11. SPUZNAC   LWITCNG   _____

12. GNCCQ   MPACL   _____

13. BWLPA   MWGFAD   _____

14. HZWWVP   TWCLRADT   _____

15. ONFZNDPEA   ZAVRIDE   _____

16. LIGFPE   ZWMMSNE   _____

17. VNIC   EAHSNE   _____

18. BNUO   EPUZWCGWE   _____

19. SADQC   GFDAAV   _____

20. LAEYAC   HNGZPETFWE   _____

DECODE EXPLORERS AND INVENTORS

Each group of letters below is a list of related names in code. Each group has its own code. Brainstorm some names to fit each category. Once you have identified a name, use the known letters to decode the other names.

Explorers

1. OELIM   _____

2. OISRVLRU   _____

3. TIBOK   PK   SKIB   _____

4. FKUTROOA   _____

5. SKZAU   EBP   OSECX   _____

6. ESKGEBPKC   MQK   NCKEM   _____

7. OICIBEPI   _____

8. LESLIE   _____

9. OECMAKC   _____

10. LDCP   _____

Inventors

11. PSYY   _____

12. TRFXDAK   _____

13. SOKBDA   _____

14. NFRAMYKA   _____

15. IWKHASG   _____

16. NEYHDA   _____

17. WDIS   _____

18. SRBHTRA   _____

19. VDDOGSRF   _____

20. VEHSAPSFV   _____

DECODE LANDMARKS AND STATES

Each group of letters below is a list of related words in code. Each group has its own code. Brainstorm some words to fit each category. Once you have identified a word, use the known letters to decode the other words.

U.S. Landmarks

1. ARLDS   VLDOCD   _____

2. TLFRHLP   LDNV   _____

3. KCBJF   DBGVKCDR   _____

4. ASPKCBFV   DCNE   _____

5. CSU   QLWFVQBS   _____

6. GFLFBR   CQ   SWORDFP   _____

7. TDLJU   NLJPCJ   _____

8. HVWFR   VCBGR   _____

9. KCBJF   KNEWJSRP   _____

10. KCBJF   GLWJF   VRSRJG   _____

U.S. States

11. FCGJN   RPECTDBP   _____

12. BQA   NPHLFNDEQ   _____

13. BCEJN   OPSCJP   _____

14. BQA   VQEFQK   _____

15. AQFJ   MDEUDBDP   _____

16. BCEJN   RPECTDBP   _____

17. BQA   KCES   _____

18. FCGJN   OPSCJP   _____

19. ENCOQ   DFTPBO   _____

20. BQA   HQIDRC   _____

DECODE SCHOOL AND MATH TERMS

Each group of letters below is a list of related words in code. Each group has its own code. Brainstorm some words to fit each category. Once you have identified a word, use the known letters to decode the other words.

School Terms

1. ADFTA _____

2. BANJWNBPF _____

3. ATWTGG _____

4. SCCHG _____

5. RPBG _____

6. BTJWNFG _____

7. KTGHG _____

8. ETPWXTA _____

9. PFRPJPW _____

10. WCRBPGG _____

Math Terms

11. AFDTRTGMGHE _____

12. PGCGKGDO _____

13. AFDPJQH _____

14. WBJRHGDO _____

15. RPPGHGDO _____

16. RFWR _____

17. KBJRFW   FDDH _____

18. PGRIWHWF _____

19. WBJGCRMWOH _____

20. IJMHGAMGQRHGDO _____

ALL FIVE VOWELS

Make a list of words that have all five vowels.

A E I O U

a   a

  _____

  _____

  _____

e _____ e

  _____

  _____

i   _____ i

  _____

  _____

o _____ o

  _____

  _____

u   u

A E I O U

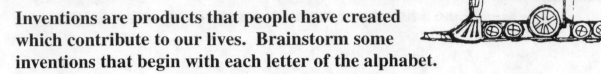

INVENTIONS

Inventions are products that people have created which contribute to our lives. Brainstorm some inventions that begin with each letter of the alphabet.

A _____   N _____
_____   _____

B _____   O _____
_____   _____

C _____   P _____
_____   _____

D _____   Q _____
_____   _____

E _____   R _____
_____   _____

F _____   S _____
_____   _____

G _____   T _____
_____   _____

H _____   U _____
_____   _____

I _____   V _____
_____   _____

J _____   W _____
_____   _____

K _____   X _____
_____   _____

L _____   Y _____
_____   _____

M _____   Z _____
_____   _____

FROM A TO Z

List as many words as you can that begin with A and end with Z, begin
with B and end with Y, and so on.

A_____Z

B_____Y

C_____X

D_____W

E_____V

F_____U

G_____T

H_____S

I_____R

J_____Q

K_____P

L_____O

M_____N

N_____M

O_____L

P_____K

Q_____J

R_____I

S_____H

T_____G

U_____F

V_____E

W_____D

X_____C

Y_____B

Z_____A

TWO OF A KIND

Make a list of words that contain two of each letter: two A's, two B's, two C's, etc. Examples are area, baby, and accent, and pudding.

A _____   N _____

_____   _____

B _____   O _____

_____   _____

C _____   P _____

_____   _____

D _____   Q _____

_____   _____

E _____   R _____

_____   _____

F _____   S _____

_____   _____

G _____   T _____

_____   _____

H _____   U _____

_____   _____

I _____   V _____

_____   _____

J _____   W _____

_____   _____

K _____   X _____

_____   _____

L _____   Y _____

_____   _____

M _____   Z _____

_____   _____

DOUBLE LETTERS

Use the following clues to find words that contain consecutive double letters.

1. A storm with wind and snow _____

2. A space with nothing in it, not even air _____

3. A sport in which touchdowns are scored _____

4. Mental ability _____

5. To draw absent-mindedly _____

6. A pirate _____

7. A winged insect, usually brightly colored _____

8. An animal with a long neck _____

9. Part of a word pronounced as a unit _____

10. Earth's natural satellite _____

11. Not guilty _____

12. A flock of geese _____

13. To move with short, quick movements; squirm _____

14. To get temporarily _____

15. Grief, sadness _____

16. To make something seem larger than it is _____

17. A sale of goods to raise funds, especially for charity _____

18. A long, tapering flag _____

19. One who expects bad things to happen _____

20. A favorable set of circumstances _____

Bonus Question:

A perplexing situation requiring a difficult choice _____

FIRST AND LAST

Each of the following clues has an answer in which the first letter is the same as the last letter.

1. An official list of names   r _ _ _ _ _ _ r

2. An amount over and above what is needed   s _ _ _ _ _ s

3. A great work of art or literature   c _ _ _ _ _ c

4. To roll about   w _ _ _ w

5. Loss of memory   a _ _ _ _ _ a

6. A state   A _ _ _ _ _ a

7. A brief advertisement   b _ _ _ b

8. Activity requiring physical exertion   e _ _ _ _ _ _ e

9. Handwriting skill   p _ _ _ _ _ _ _ _ p

10. A word used by magicians   a _ _ _ _ _ _ _ _ _ _ a

11. To rub out   e _ _ _ e

12. A continent   A _ _ _ _ _ _ _ a

13. A bird   e _ _ _ e

14. Willing to let others do as they want   t _ _ _ _ _ _ t

15. Having made twice as much   d _ _ _ _ _ d

16. A horizontal beam above a door or window   l _ _ _ _ l

17. An edible seed of a bean plant   l _ _ _ _ l

18. The act or words of welcoming someone   g _ _ _ _ _ _ g

19. One thousand years   m _ _ _ _ _ _ _ _ m

20. To regain health after illness   r _ _ _ _ _ r

Bonus Question:

A summary   s _ _ _ _ _ _ s

SIMILES

Similes are figures of speech stating that one thing is like another. An
example is "as fresh as a daisy." Complete the following similes.
Then write five additional similes.

1. As sharp as a _____.

2. As stubborn as a _____.

3. As flat as a _____.

4. As happy as a _____.

5. As hard as _____.

6. As blind as a _____.

7. As sly as a _____.

8. As cold as _____.

9. As clean as a _____.

10. As quick as a _____.

11. As light as a _____.

12. As black as _____.

13. As limp as a _____.

14. As cool as a _____.

15. As stiff as a _____.

16. _____

17. _____

18. _____

19. _____

20. _____

PROVERBS

Proverbs are old, familiar sayings that often give advice for daily living. Complete each of the following proverbs and explain what it means.

1. Early to bed and early to rise _____

   _____

2. Don't count your chickens _____

   _____

3. Birds of a feather _____

   _____

4. When the cat's away, _____

   _____

5. Look before _____

   _____

6. The early bird _____

   _____

7. Don't look a gift horse _____

   _____

8. A penny saved _____

   _____

9. Never put off till tomorrow _____

   _____

10. Haste makes _____

    _____

MORE PROVERBS

Proverbs are old, familiar sayings that often give advice for daily living. Complete each of the following proverbs and explain what it means.

1. Two wrongs _____

_____

2. Actions speak _____

_____

3. Don't cry over _____

_____

4. A stitch in time _____

_____

5. You can't teach an old dog _____

_____

6. A friend in need _____

_____

7. The grass is always greener _____

_____

8. A bird in the hand _____

_____

9. Two heads _____

_____

10. All that glitters _____

_____

WHAT DOES IT MEAN?

Explain the meaning of each word or phrase below.

1. Heebie-jeebies _____

2. Bon appétit _____

3. Oodles _____

4. A black sheep _____

5. A ballpark figure _____

6. Vamoose _____

7. Riffraff _____

8. Once in a blue moon _____

9. Eat crow _____

10. A la carte _____

11. Crocodile tears _____

12. Wishy-washy _____

13. Bon voyage _____

14. Gracias _____

15. Mañana _____

16. Cold feet _____

17. Cold shoulder _____

18. Touché _____

19. Shipshape _____

20. Forty winks _____

KNOW NOSE EXPRESSIONS

Demonstrate that you know these nose expressions
by writing their meanings on the blanks below.

1. On the nose _____

   _____

2. To look down one's nose at _____

   _____

3. Under one's nose _____

   _____

4. To pay through the nose _____

   _____

5. To follow one's nose_____

   _____

6. To stick one's nose in _____

   _____

7. To put someone's nose out of joint _____

   _____

8. To win by a nose _____

   _____

9. To turn up one's nose at _____

   _____

10. To cut off one's nose to spite one's face _____

   _____

INEDIBLE FOOD

The following expressions refer to food, but they don't have anything to do with eating. Explain what the following expressions mean.

1. The apple of one's eye _____

2. To ham it up _____

3. Cool as a cucumber _____

4. Full of baloney _____

5. Meat and potatoes _____

6. To bring home the bacon _____

7. To talk turkey _____

8. High on the hog _____

9. Egg on one's face _____

10. To cook one's own goose _____

11. Full of beans _____

12. A rotten egg _____

13. A hot dog _____

14. To cook up _____

15. To take it with a grain of salt _____

BODY LANGUAGE

Fill in the blanks with the names of parts of the body.

1. By the skin of one's _____.

2. _____ and _____ above the rest.

3. Keep a stiff upper _____.

4. A lump in the _____.

5. Don't stick your _____ out.

6. Nothing but _____ and _____.

7. Out on a _____.

8. Pot_____ stove.

9. A _____ watch.

10. See _____ to _____.

11. With your _____ to the wall.

12. To go in one _____ and out the other.

13. Get to the _____ of the matter.

14. All _____ on deck.

15. Get a _____ in the door.

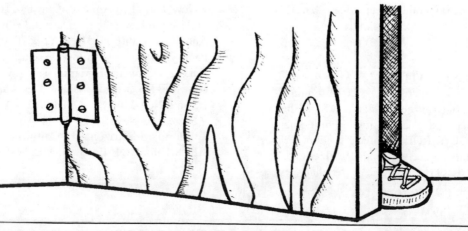

ANSWER KEY

Page 3, FAMOUS QUOTATIONS
1 William Shakespeare. 2 John Paul Jones. 3-Franklin D.
Roosevelt. 4-Marie Antoinette. 5-Martin Luther King, Jr.
6-Patrick Henry. 7-Neil A. Armstrong. 8-Robert Frost.
9-John F. Kennedy. 10-Will Rogers. 11-Abraham Lincoln.
12-Benjamin Franklin. 13-Yogi Berra. 14-Thomas
Jefferson. 15-Harry S. Truman.

Page 4, INVENTORS AND THEIR INVENTIONS
1-telephone. 2-sewing machine. 3-dynamite. 4-cotton gin.
5-quick-freezing process of preserving food. 6-assembly
line method of production. 7-vulcanization of rubber.
8-electric light. 9-wireless telegraph. 10-first successful
airplane. 11-printing from movable type. 12-steel plow.
13-railroad sleeping car. 14-bifocal glasses. 15-Kodak
camera.

Page 5, FAMOUS AMERICANS
1-Francis Scott Key. 2-Betsy Ross. 3-Jefferson Davis.
4-Clara Barton. 5-George Washington Carver. 6-Sitting
Bull. 7-Daniel Boone. 8-P. T. Barnum. 9-Johnny
Appleseed (or John Chapman). 10-Susan B. Anthony.
11-Jackie Robinson. 12-Jim Thorpe. 13-Benjamin
Franklin. 14-Louisa May Alcott. 15-Ernest Hemingway.

Page 6, U.S. PRESIDENTS
1-George Washington. 2-Lyndon B. Johnson. 3-Richard
M. Nixon. 4-George Washington. 5-Dwight D.
Eisenhower. 6-Grover Cleveland. 7-John Adams, John
Quincy Adams. 8-Calvin Coolidge. 9-Grover Cleveland.
10-Franklin D. Roosevelt. 11-William H. Taft.
12-William H. Taft. 13-John Tyler. 14-William Henry
Harrison. 15-Theodore Roosevelt. 16-Abraham Lincoln.
17-Zachary Taylor. 18-Thomas Jefferson.

Page 7, FAMOUS FIRSTS
1-Alan Shepard Jr. 2-Sally Ride. 3-John Glenn Jr.
4-Edward H. White II. 5-Neil Armstrong. 6-George
Washington. 7-John Adams. 8-Victoria Woodhull.
9-Abraham Lincoln. 10-Geraldine Ferraro. 11-Virginia
Dare. 12-John Hancock. 13-Marian Anderson.
14-Elizabeth Blackwell. 15-Charles Yeager.

Page 8, CONTINENT MATCH
AFRICA-Egypt, Libya, Algeria, Morocco, Ethiopia,
Sudan, Kenya, Nigeria, Tanzania, Angola. ASIA-China,
Japan, India, Vietnam, Iran, Saudi Arabia, Philippines,
Israel, Iraq, Thailand. EUROPE-United Kingdom, France,
Germany, Spain, Italy, Greece, Sweden, Switzerland,
Poland, Hungary. NORTH AMERICA-Greenland,
Canada, United States, Mexico, Cuba, Costa Rica,
Nicaragua, Panama, El Salvador, Guatemala. SOUTH
AMERICA-Brazil, Uruguay, Argentina, Chile, Bolivia,
Peru, Ecuador, Colombia, Venezuela, Paraguay.

Page 9, NAME THE COUNTRIES
1-Canada. 2-Ireland. 3-India. 4-Egypt. 5-Japan. 6-Brazil.
7-Germany. 8-China. 9-Sweden. 10-France. 11-Mexico.
12-Spain. 13-Australia. 14-South Africa. 15-Morocco.
16-Argentina. 17-United Kingdom. 18-Italy. 19-Russia.
20-Austria.

Page 10, LANDMARKS
1-London. 2-Rome. 3-Paris. 4-San Francisco. 5-Egypt.
6-India. 7-St. Louis. 8-Athens, Greece. 9-New York City.
10-China. 11-Seattle. 12-Denmark. 13-Mexico.
14-Moscow. 15-Houston.

Page 11, STATE CAPITALS

Page 12, U.S. CITIES, STATES, AND PARKS
1-New York, Los Angeles, Chicago, Houston,
Philadelphia, San Diego, Detroit, Dallas, Phoenix, San
Antonio. 2-California, New York, Texas, Florida,
Pennsylvania. 3-Wyoming, Alaska, Vermont, North
Dakota, Delaware. 4-Alaska, Texas, California, Montana,
New Mexico. 5-Rhode Island, Delaware, Connecticut,
Hawaii, New Jersey. 6-Oklahoma. 7-Iowa. 8-Kentucky.
9-Maine. 10-Nevada. 11-South Dakota. 12-Oregon.
13-Florida. 14-Arizona. 15-California. Bonus: N-Barrow,
AK. S-Hilo, HI. E-Eastport, ME. W-West Unalaska, AK.

ANSWER KEY (continued)

Page 13, SPECIFIC GROUPS
1-American League baseball teams. 2-NFC football teams. 3-Vegetables that grow underground. 4-Citrus fruits. 5-Fruits that begin with the letter P. 6-Months with 30 days. 7-Candy bars with nuts. 8-Members of the cat family. 9-Mythical creatures. 10-Ground transportation. 11-Republican Presidents. 12-Democratic Presidents. 13-States that border the Gulf of Mexico. 14-States that border the Atlantic Ocean. 15-States that border Mexico. Bonus: States whose entire eastern borders are formed by the Mississippi River.

Page 14, WHICH ONE DOESN'T BELONG?
1-Bartlett, varieties of apples. 2-niece, males. 3-math, reference materials. 4-maple, flowers. 5-chicken, animals with four legs. 6-eraser, tools for writing or drawing. 7-green, primary colors. 8-angora, breeds of dogs. 9-calculus, clouds. 10-acre, metric measures. Bonus: sphere, plane (flat) figures.

Page 15, ANIMAL FAMILIES AND GROUPS
cattle-bull, cow, calf, herd (or drove)
sheep-ram, ewe (or dam), lamb, flock
seal-bull, cow, pup, herd
kangaroo-buck, doe, joey, herd
hog-boar, sow, piglet, herd
lion-lion, lioness, cub, pride
ostrich-cock, hen, chick, flock
whale-bull, cow, calf, herd
chicken-rooster, hen, chick, flock
goat-billy (or buck), nanny, kid, herd
goose-gander, goose, gosling, gaggle
fox-dog, vixen, cub, skulk

Page 16, WORD TWINS
1-saucer. 2-forth. 3-down. 4-sound. 5-bolts. 6-thin. 7-fork. 8-beans. 9-no. 10-write. 11-found. 12-pains. 13-water. 14-go (or think). 15-learn (or let live). 16-pepper. 17-stones. 18-turn. 19-low (or dry or mighty). 20-then. 21-bad (or ready). 22-wrong. 23-right. 24-dance. 25-listen. 26-white (or blue). 27-go. 28-needles. 29-nail. 30-go. 31-eggs. 32-cheese. 33-butter (or water). 34-potatoes. 35-onions. 36-gravy. 37-joy. 38-proper. 39-foot. 40-nails (or sickle).

Page 17, FAMILY VACATION
Tuesday-Sea World
Wednesday-Universal Studios Florida
Thursday-Orlando Science Center
Friday-Walt Disney World
Saturday-EPCOT Center

Page 18, THUNDERSTORM CONFUSION
1-cow. 2-rabbits. 3-horse. 4-sheep. 5-goat. 6-pig.

Page 19, BASEBALL BATTING ORDER
1-Alex. 2-Dan. 3-Todd. 4-Jakob. 5-Emilio. 6-Phil. 7-Henrik. 8-Amos. 9-Bill.

Page 20, FAVORITE TEAMS
Chad-Reds. Dave-Cubs. Adam-White Sox. Ryan-Dodgers, Will-A's.

Page 23, ART, MUSIC, LITERATURE
1-*Mona Lisa*. 2-Sistine Chapel. 3-impressionism. 4-*American Gothic*. 5-photography. 6-Beatles. 7-Duke Ellington. 8-*The Nutcracker*. 9-*Aida*. 10-Beethoven. 11-Langston Hughes. 12-Jane Austen. 13-Charles Dickens. 14-Edgar Allan Poe. 15-Mark Twain.

Page 24, HIDDEN MEANINGS
1-checkup. 2-going on a diet. 3-long time, no see. 4-man overboard. 5-scatterbrained. 6-tricycle. 7-holy cow. 8-GI overseas. 9-H_2O. 10-One in a million. 11-touchdown. 12-split decision.

Page 25, MORE HIDDEN MEANINGS
1-circles under the eyes. 2-square meal. 3-just in time. 4-half an hour. 5-Big Mac™. 6-Six feet under ground. 7-banana split. 8-man in the moon. 9-long underwear. 10-hole in one. 11-three degrees above zero. 12-all mixed up or all around.

Page 27, ADD AND SUBTRACT
1. $3+5-3+9+6-5-4+2=13$
2. $9+8+1+2-9-6+8-8=5$
3. $1+6+3+7-9-4+5+7=16$
4. $6+3-2+8+5+7-4-6=17$
5. $2-1+8+9-4-9+7-2=10$
6. $5+8-2-7+3+6+2-9=6$
7. $5-3+5+4-4+2+9-8=10$
8. $7+6+2+9-9-3+7-2=17$
9. $6+3+8+3-2-5+2-9=6$
10. $4+9-6-5+2+8-4-1=7$

Page 28, NUMBERS, NUMBERS, NUMBERS
1-4. 2-5. 3-9. 4-1. 5-32. 6-8. 7-1. 8-90. 9-5. 10-8. 11-1. 12-3. 13-3. 14-10. 15-4. 16-1. 17-16. 18-110. 19-4. 20-0.

Page 29, CALCULATOR SPELLING
1-ho, ho, ho. 2-loose. 3-sob. 4-oil. 5-hose. 6-less. 7-shoe. 8-big. 9-boil. 10-soil. 11-beg. 12-Bob. 13-go. 14-hole. 15-giggle.

ANSWER KEY (continued)

Page 30, EQUATIONS

1-voices in a trio. 2-quarts in a gallon. 3-sides of a hexagon. 4-players on a football team. 5-eggs in a dozen. 6-inches in a foot. 7-ounces in a pound. 8-years in a score. 9-cards in a deck. 10-seconds in a minute. 11-minutes in an hour. 12-squares on a checkerboard. 13-years in a century. 14-pennies in a dollar. 15-items in a gross. 16-degrees in a circle. 17-days in a leap year. 18-millimeters in a meter. 19-pounds in a ton. 20-feet in a mile.

Page 31, TRIVIA TIME

1-Alexander Hamilton's. 2-moon. 3-5 or 9. 4-4. 5-maximum. 6-down. 7-numerator. 8-red. 9-tennis. 10-Genesis. 11-Left. 12-Saturn. 13-42. 14-64. 15-west. 16-princess. 17-red, yellow, green. 18-caboose. 19-eye. 20-copper-coated zinc.

Page 32, SCIENCE TRIVIA

1-fog. 2-microscope. 3-Jupiter. 4-barometer. 5-tadpole. 6-diamond. 7-smog. 8-skunk. 9-muscles. 10-8. 11-ribs. 12-98.6°F. 13-Earth. 14-hummingbird. 15-elbow. 16-deciduous. 17-chlorophyll. 18-circulatory. 19-iris. 20-software.

Page 33, U.S. TRIVIA

1-Christopher Columbus. 2-John Wilkes Booth. 3-Hawaii. 4-Old Glory or The Stars and Stripes. 5-Declaration of Independence. 6-In God We Trust. 7-defending the Alamo. 8-Robert E. Lee. 9-Ulysses S. Grant. 10-Super Bowl. 11-Revolutionary War. 12-Civil War. 13-Buffalo Bill. 14-baseball. 15-FBI. 16-June 6, 1944. 17-Revolutionary War. 18-Richard Nixon. 19-Constitution. 20-National Aeronautics and Space Administration.

Page 34, WHICH IS IT?

1-12. 2-4 sides. 3-Utah. 4-3rd President. 5-50 states. 6-Washington, D.C. 7-12 months. 8-24 hours. 9-10 years. 10-132. 11-12 sides. 12-13. 13-over 600. 14-November. 15-Austin. 16-Lincoln. 17-cumulus. 18-Florida. 19-tambourine. 20-Picasso.

Page 35, THE LARGEST TO THE SMALLEST

1-Greenland. 2-Chihuahua. 3-Lake Superior. 4-Andes. 5-Australia. 6-anaconda. 7-South China Sea. 8-Russia. 9-Mt. Everest. 10-blue whale. 11-Pacific. 12-Nile. 13-Sahara. 14-cheetah. 15-bee hummingbird.

Page 36, ACRONYMS

1-very important person. 2-Internal Revenue Service. 3-tender loving care. 4-knock out. 5-cash on delivery. 6-prisoner of war. 7-district attorney. 8-disk jockey. 9-missing in action. 10-American Association of Retired Persons. 11-North Atlantic Treaty Organization. 12-intelligence quotient. 13-video display terminal. 14-United Nations Educational, Scientific, and Cultural Organization. 15-Society for the Prevention of Cruelty to Animals. Bonus: répondez s'il vous plaît (please reply). first in, first out.

Page 37, ANTONYMS, HOMOPHONES, SYNONYMS

1-homophone. 2-antonym. 3-synonym. 4-antonym. 5-synonym. 6-antonym. 7-homophone. 8-synonym. 9-synonym. 10-synonym. 11-homophone. 12-synonym. 13-antonym. 14-homophone. 14-synonym. 16-homophone. 17-synonym. 18-antonym. 19-synonym. 20-antonym.

Page 38, IF AND WHERE TO USE THE HYPHEN

1-jack-o'-lantern. 2-nontransferable. 3-autobiography. 4-brother-in-law. 5-once-over. 6-undergraduate. 7-attorney general. 8-old-fashioned. 9-left-handed. 10-all ready. 11-hide-and-seek. 12-weather bureau. 13-two-thirds. 14-coauthor. 15-know-it-all. 16-thirty-nine. 17-out-of-date. 18-open-ended. 19-two-by-four. 20-ongoing.

Page 39, SHORT FORM/LONG FORM

1-gasoline. 2-mathematics. 3-limousine. 4-doctor. 5-refrigerator. 6-hamburger. 7-airplane. 8-laboratory. 9-automobile. 10-examination. 11-referee. 12-champion. 13-graduate. 14-submarine. 15-telephone.

Page 40, RHYMING WORD PAIRS

1-shy fly. 2-roast toast. 3-glum chum. 4-fat cat. 5-fender bender. 6-pale male. 7-big pig. 8-sick chick. 9-fat rat. 10-grand band. 11-light bite. 12-fun run. 13-wet pet. 14-gory story. 15-double trouble. 16-sick tick. 17-pink drink. 18-wee flea. 19-witty kitty. 20-sad lad.

Page 41, WHICH WORD?

1-effect. 2-angel. 3-latter. 4-accept. 5-quit. 6-anyway. 7-illicit. 8-stationery. 9-thorough. 10-proceed. 11-disprove. 12-preposition. 13-imply. 14-capital. 15-desert.

Page 42, WORD CHAIN

1-zebra. 2-rattan. 3-answer. 4-erase. 5-several. 6-Alabama. 7-macaroni. 8-niece. 9-centipede. 10-decline. 11-negative. 12-verse. 13-seal. 14-alley. 15-eye. 16-year. 17-architecture. 18-recipe. 19-pedestrian. 20-anxious.

ANSWER KEY (continued)

Page 44, WORD WINDERS
1-sharp. 2-share. 3-care. 4-cart. 5-chart. 6-charm. 7-hard. 8-hare. 9-fare. 10-farm. 11-alarm. 12-lark. 13-bark. 14-dark. 15-dare. 16-date. 17-late. 18-lane. 19-cane. 20-cone.

Page 45, ONE WORD PLUS ANOTHER
1-rot, ate, rotate. 2-don, key, donkey. 3-par, take, partake. 4-car, pet, carpet. 5-bud, get, budget. 6-leg, end, legend. 7-win, try, wintry. 8-ash, ore, ashore.

Page 46, LETTER ANSWERS
1-EZ. 2-C. 3-O. 4-B. 5-T. 6-P. 7-Y. 8-K. 9-IV. 10-TP. 11-CU. 12-I. 13-DJ. 14-IC. 15-U.

Page 47, COLORFUL WORDS
1-pinkeye. 2-Blackbeard. 3-orange. 4-Purple Heart. 5-greenhorn. 6-red meat. 7-bluebird. 8-whitewall. 9-green pepper. 10-blackboard. 11-violet. 12-Greyhound. 13-brownie. 14-yellow jacket. 15-Golden Gate Bridge.

Page 48, RE"CON"STRUCT THESE WORDS
1-conceal. 2-continents. 3-reconcile. 4-concert. 5-consonants. 6-condiments. 7-conclusion. 8-concoct. 9-pros and cons. 10-confused. 11-congratulate. 12-continue. 13-concrete. 14-Connecticut. 15-confetti.

Page 49, ARE YOU A WORD "FAN"?
1-infantry. 2-flannel. 3-fanatic. 4-filament. 5-fan mail. 6-fantastic. 7-fanfare. 8-fancy. 9-fantail. 10-famine. 11-fancy-free. 12-fantasy. 13-falling star. 14-infant. 15-fangs.

Page 50, NO! NO! A THOUSAND TIMES NO!
1-knowledge. 2-noose. 3-novel. 4-nonsense. 5-nose. 6-gnome. 7-noodle. 8-nomad. 9-snout. 10-equinox. 11-nobody. 12-knock. 13-noise. 14-Noah. 15-Knoxville.

Page 51, "CAR" PARTS OF WORDS
1-cartoons. 2-Cardinals. 3-carton. 4-cardigan. 5-carpet. 6-carburetor. 7-discard. 8-carnation. 9-carnival. 10-carousel. 11-caricature. 12-incarcerate. 13-carnivores. 14-caramel. 15-carat.

Page 52, "THE" WORDS
1-thermometer. 2-theft. 3-theater. 4-bathe. 5-thesaurus. 6-mathematics. 7-weather. 8-panther. 9-theme song. 10-thesis. 11-thereabouts. 12-then. 13-theory. 14-gather. 15-thermostat.

Page 53, "BLACK" IS BEAUTIFUL
1-blacktop. 2-black-eyed pea. 3-blackberry. 4-blackmail. 5-black widow. 6-black-and-blue. 7-black gold. 8-blackjack. 9-black hole. 10-black market. 11-black belt. 12-Blackbeard. 13-black sheep. 14-Black Hills. 15-black-eyed Susan.

Page 54, "CATS" AND "DOGS"
1-catalog. 2-dog paddle. 3-cathedral. 4-dog tag. 5-catastrophe. 6-dog-tired. 7-cattails. 8-hot dog. 9-caterpillar. 10-underdog. 11-cat nap. 12-dog-eared. 13-catcher. 14-dogwood. 15-catamaran.

Page 55, "HEADS" OR "TAILS"
1-head start. 2-tailgate. 3-headline. 4-tailor. 5-headquarters. 6-tail light. 7-headstrong. 8-tail end. 9-headway. 10-tail spin. 11-headmaster. 12-tailback. 13-head-to-toe. 14-tail pipe. 15-headlight.

Page 56, PUTTING THE PIECES TOGETHER
Group 1: carpenter, disobey, allowance, estimate, fiesta, hemisphere, microwave, nucleus, parallel, reconstruct.
Group 2: boundary, government, impressive, livelihood, official, specialize, tragedy, unravel, vigorous, wonderful.

Page 57, WEATHER WORDS
1-icy. 2-thunder. 3-heat. 4-season. 5-sun. 6-cloud. 7-warm. 8-tornado. 9-clear. 10-rain. 11-cold. 12-hot. 13-wind. 14-hail. 15-snow.

Page 58, CODED MESSAGE
1-F. 2-O. 3-N. 4-H. 5-A. 6-U. 7-Y. 8-C. 9-T. 10-K. 11-I.

Page 59, DECODE AUTHORS AND ACTORS
1-Louisa May Alcott. 2-Hans Christian Andersen. 3-Judy Blume. 4-Beverly Cleary. 5-Charles Dickens. 6-Emily Dickinson. 7-Nathaniel Hawthorne. 8-William Shakespeare. 9-Mark Twain. 10-Laura Ingalls Wilder. 11-Michael Douglas. 12-Sally Field. 13-Jodie Foster. 14-Whoopi Goldberg. 15-Katharine Hepburn. 16-Dustin Hoffman. 17-Paul Newman. 18-Jack Nicholson. 19-Meryl Streep. 20-Denzel Washington.

Page 60, DECODE EXPLORERS AND INVENTORS
1-Cabot. 2-Columbus. 3-Ponce de Leon. 4-Vespucci. 5-Lewis and Clark. 6-Alexander the Great. 7-Coronado. 8-Balboa. 9-Cartier. 10-Byrd. 11-Bell. 12-Marconi. 13-Edison. 14-Franklin. 15-Whitney. 16-Fulton. 17-Howe. 18-Eastman. 19-Goodyear. 20-Gutenberg.

ANSWER KEY (continued)

Page 61, DECODE LANDMARKS AND STATES
1-Pearl Harbor. 2-Gateway Arch. 3-Mount Rushmore.
4-Plymouth Rock. 5-Old Faithful. 6-Statue of Liberty.
7-Grand Canyon. 8-White House. 9-Mount McKinley.
10-Mount Saint Helens. 11-South Carolina. 12-New
Hampshire. 13-North Dakota. 14-New Jersey. 15-West
Virginia. 16-North Carolina. 17-New York. 18-South
Dakota. 19-Rhode Island. 20-New Mexico.

Page 62, DECODE SCHOOL AND MATH TERMS
1-ruler. 2-principal. 3-recess. 4-books. 5-maps. 6-pencils.
7-desks. 8-teacher. 9-almanac. 10-compass.
11-probability. 12-division. 13-product. 14-equation.
15-addition. 16-area. 17-square root. 18-diameter.
19-equivalent. 20-multiplication.

Page 63, ALL FIVE VOWELS
Possible answers include dialogue, auctioned, housemaid,
cautioned, reputation, equation, overhauling, pneumonia,
discourage, uncomplimentary, ambidextrous,
encouraging, unquestionably, ultraviolet, facetious.

Page 65, FROM A TO Z
Answers will vary. Many answers will be difficult to find,
and some will be impossible. This page may be
approached as a competitive group activity.

Page 67, DOUBLE LETTERS
1-blizzard. 2-vacuum. 3-football. 4-intelligence. 5-doodle.
6-buccaneer. 7-butterfly. 8-giraffe. 9-syllable. 10-moon.
11-innocent. 12-gaggle. 13-wiggle. 14-borrow. 15-sorrow.
16-exaggerate. 17-bazaar. 18-pennant. 19-pessimist.
20-opportunity. Bonus: dilemma.

Page 68, FIRST AND LAST
1-register. 2-surplus. 3-classic. 4-wallow. 5-amnesia.
6-Alabama. 7-blurb. 8-exercise. 9-penmanship.
10-abracadabra. 11-erase. 12-Australia. 13-eagle.
14-tolerant. 15-doubled. 16-lintel. 17-lentil. 18-greeting.
19-millennium. 20-recover. Bonus: synopsis.

Page 69, SIMILES
1-tack. 2-mule. 3-pancake. 4-lark. 5-nails. 6-bat. 7-fox.
8-ice. 9-whistle. 10-wink. 11-feather. 12-night. 13-wet
noodle. 14-cucumber. 15-board.

Page 70, PROVERBS
1. makes a man healthy, wealthy, and wise. 2-before they
hatch. 3-flock together. 4-the mice will play. 5-you leap.
6-catches the worm. 7-in the mouth. 8-is a penny earned.
9-what you can do today. 10-waste.

Page 71, MORE PROVERBS
1-don't make a right. 2-louder than words. 3-spilt milk. 4-
saves nine. 5-new tricks. 6-is a friend indeed. 7-on the
other side. 8-is worth two in the bush. 9-are better than
one. 10-is not gold.

Page 72, WHAT DOES IT MEAN?
1-extreme nervousness. 2-French for good eating or good
appetite. 3-lots. 4-a bad character in an otherwise well-
behaved group. 5-an estimate. 6-go away quickly. 7-
people regarded as worthless. 8-very rarely. 9-to be
forced to admit something humiliating. 10-with a separate
price for each dish. 11-a show of insincere grief. 12-weak;
lacking strength. 13-good-by; have a good trip. 14-
Spanish for thank you. 15-tomorrow; sometime. 16-a lack
of confidence; a change of mind. 17-deliberately
unfriendly treatment. 18-an acknowledgment of a good
point in an argument or a clever reply. 19-neat and in
order. 20-a short nap.

Page 73, KNOW NOSE EXPRESSIONS
1-exactly. 2-to treat with scorn or contempt. 3-in plain
sight. 4-to pay an exorbitant price. 5-to go straight ahead.
6-to interfere. 7-to make someone feel slighted. 8-to win
by a small margin. 9-to treat with scorn or contempt. 10-
to do something harmful to someone else knowing that it
is to one's own detriment.

Page 74, INEDIBLE FOOD
1-person or thing that is adored or cherished. 2-to overact;
overplay. 3-calm. 4-not reliable; full of nonsense. 5-the
basics. 6-to earn an income. 7-to talk frankly. 8-lavishly.
9-humiliation. 10-to destroy one's plan or one's
reputation. 11-lively; peppy. 12-a bad person. 13-a show-
off in sports or an exclamation. 14-to create or to prepare
falsely. 15-to believe only in part.

Page 75, BODY LANGUAGE
1-teeth. 2-head, shoulders. 3-lip. 4-throat. 5-neck. 6-skin,
bones. 7-limb. 8-belly. 9-wrist. 10-eye, eye. 11-back. 12-
ear. 13-heart. 14-hands. 15-foot.